WHEN Sheffielders turned out in their hundreds one rainy Saturday night in October 1960 to say good-bye to their trams, they were taking part in the end of almost ninety years of Sheffield's history. Fondly remembered by most people, Sheffield's blue and cream trams have left an indelible mark on the City. Stand on the corner of Fitzalan Square and High Street today and most of the bright red and cream buses you'll see still quietly follow the routes established long ago by electric trams, to Crookes, Walkley and Intake, Fulwood and Nether Edge, and north to Sheffield Lane Top and Rotherham.

It was in 1873 that Sheffield's first horse tramway was opened from Lady's Bridge to the *Golden Ball Hotel*, Attercliffe Common. Before that time a limited network of horse bus services had appeared, but they were expensive and ran only in the more wealthy suburbs. Tram fares were cheaper right from the start, and remained so. By 1877 trams were running to Tinsley and Brightside, from Snig Hill to Hillsborough, and from Moorhead to Nether Edge and Heeley, but none of them passed through the town centre.

Early trams were either one-horse single-deckers or two-horse open-topped double-deckers: a single-deck car is preserved at the Crich Tram Museum. For a while in 1878 a steam tram ran on the Brightside route, but the smoking chimney was unpopular. Horse trams were owned by the Sheffield Tramways Company, but in 1896 Sheffield Corporation — which already owned the track — took over the trams as well. On 5 September 1899 electric trams began running between Tinsley and Nether Edge along the former horse-car routes, and the steady plod of the horse was replaced by the more powerful electric motor, with passengers being carried at greater speed, in greater comfort and right across the centre of town. At night the trams were ablaze with light, which must have been quite a sight in those oil and gas-lit days.

The Victorian era was the railway age, but looking back we can see that the Victorians made little attempt to provide their growing towns and cities with good cheap transport for the working classes. The Edwardians more than made up for this, and by the end of Edward VII's reign in 1910 Sheffield had a network of thirty-nine miles of tram route radiating from the city centre, on which operated 264 trams. Fares were down to one penny, which gave many families the opportunity to travel for the first time and thus move out of the densely-built back-to-back houses around the city centre and in the smoke-laden valley bottoms in the east end. So the habit of travelling from home to work was established on a wide scale.

Graham Hague and Howard Turner

First published in 1987 by Sheaf Publishing Ltd, 35 Moorooaks Road, Sheffield S10 1BX

© Sheaf Publishing 1987

Typeset in 9pt Clearface and Gill Bold and printed in Sheffield

ISBN 1 85048 006 0

Many of the photographs in this book were taken by Howard Turner. Others were kindly supplied by Sheffield City Council's Director of Land and Planning and Messrs C. Carter, R.F. Mack, R.B. Parr, H.B. Priestley and R.J.S Wiseman. To them and to everyone who helped with the preparation of this book the authors offer their grateful thanks.

Sheffield's first electric trams were open-toppers, carrying fifty-one passengers, twenty-two of them on two long wooden benches in the lower saloon. Between 1899 and 1904, 172 such trams were built, many in Sheffield by Craven's of Darnall and by the Corporation in its own Queen's Road workshops. Between 1903 and 1913 all were fitted with top-deck roofs. In early years large letters were fitted to the ends of trams to show their destination, for not everyone could read in those days. Tram 225 stands by the Crimea Monument at Moorhead bound for Norton Woodseats (N) in 1902.

Most tram routes were extended at intervals as Sheffield's population grew and the suburbs spread. In some cases routes were extended to encourage development along the tracks. By 1914 trams were running to Tinsley and Rotherham: Brightside, Firth Park and Grimesthorpe (Petre Street was a curious route that only lasted until 1925); Hillsborough, Middlewood and Malin Bridge; Crookes and Walkley; Nether Green, Banner Cross and Nether Edge; Millhouses and Woodseats; Woodhouse Road and just beyond Manor Top. Sheffield's tram map was almost complete.

The First World War did great things for the development of the motor bus, and from 1918 onwards it was buses rather than trams which developed still-growing Sheffield. A few tram extensions were built, in 1922 to Ecclesall, in 1923 to Fulwood and Woodseats (Abbey Lane), in 1924 to Wadsley Bridge, in 1927 to Beachief and up Abbey Lane, and in 1928 to Meadowhead and along the length of Prince of Wales Road. But the place of trams in the City's inter-war growth was too often neglected.

Virtually unplanned, semi-detached villas sprawled rapidly in the suburbs, linking the City with outlying areas. Tram routes were not generally extended to serve them, and these new housing developments were built in a way that did not really justify them. Low-density housing does not warrant the frequent services that trams can provide so economically; the ten-minute tram service on Abbey Lane could hardly have been worth-while.

Sixty-nine single-deck electric trams were built between 1899 and 1904, for use on hilly routes on which it was believed double-deckers would be unsafe. Some were later rebuilt as double-deckers.

At the same time, a good many Corporation housing estates were built away from tram routes, and few attempts were made to extend existing services to reach them. The tracks were not extended from Malin Bridge to Wisewood, or to Shiregreen or Parson Cross; bus services were put on instead which inevitably competed with the trams. The Edwardian initiative was ruined by poor forward-planning and muddled thinking.

By 1928 the golden days of trams in this country were over. In 1934 the routes to Handsworth and Firth Park were extened, to Orgreave Lane and Sheffield Lane Top, and at the end of 1935 the very last route extension — to Intake terminus — was opened. But already in 1934 the route to Nether Edge had closed and nearby Rotherham had shut its last tram service (apart from the through route to Sheffield).

Middlewood terminus around 1920, at the entrance to the hospital. Tram 316 was built in 1913 by Brush of Loughborough, a well-known tram builder. The driver now has a glass screen protecting him from the weather, but the upstairs balconies remain open, enjoyable in summer but shunned in the winter. It was at terminals like this that bus services connected with outlying areas, such as Stocksbridge.

After the First World War, Sheffield Corporation began re-building seventy-five trams with glazed balconies and platforms. Four completely new trams were also built to a similar appearance and, between 1919 and 1927, 150 new trams were built to replace older vehicles.

Sixty-seven new trams with domed roofs were built by Sheffield Corporation between 1936 and 1939. This design was also used for fourteen trams built between 1941 and 1944 to replace war-damaged vehicles.

Throughout both World Wars, and particularly during the Second, because the bus depended on imported fuel rather than home-produced coal, tram services played an important part in maintaining Sheffield's industrial war effort, although bombing raids on 12th and 15th December 1940 brought the system to a halt from which it took two months to completely recover.

Sheffield's trams had always been fairly standard-looking four-wheelers, but in 1946 the Transport Department built a brand new tram, numbered 501, the first of thirty-six which became known as the Roberts cars. They were splendid vehicles, smooth, modern-looking trams, but the pity was that before the last one went into service in 1952 the City Council had already decided to replace all Sheffield's trams with buses. With hindsight we can see that this was a silly decision, but at the time it was believed that trams caused traffic congestion and that everybody would soon own a car. And because trams were steadily going from most large towns and cities in Britain, spares, fittings and the trams themselves were becoming hard to obtain.

Throughout the 1950s, route-by-route buses replaced trams, but the surviving tracks were well-maintained and the trams kept their smart appearance. By the summer of 1960 the only routes left were from High Street to Beauchief and Vulcan Road. On 8th October, they, too were replaced by buses, leaving trams running only in Blackpool and Glasgow.

In the pages that follow, we take you on a trip around Sheffield's tram routes as they were in the years after 1935. You'll find a find a few diversions into odd corners, and stops to examine some tramway rarity. Finally we look at the trams' departure from Sheffield and what they've left behind them. For although the City Council has approved the building of Super-trams, the days of blue and cream double-deck Sheffield trams are well and truly over.

Between 1928 and 1936, 212 'standard' trams were built. Attractive and functional to look at, they had upholstered seats throughout, with forward-facing seats in the lower saloon instead of the long benches that had been normal up until then. Some were still in use in 1960.

Sheffield's last new trams were the attractive and - for their day, very modern - Roberts cars, thirty-six of which were bought between 1946 and 1952.

The Wicker and Waingate

Under the Wicker Arch on 19 June 1937 (left), the familiar traffic policeman is allowing five cyclists the right of way. Tram 479, built by Craven's of Darnall in 1926 and bound for Tinsley, looks next to move. Note the line of attractive posters under the arch. The viaduct was built by the Manchester, Sheffield and Lincolnshire Railway and opened in 1849.

South of Wicker Arches (below) a week later, and this time the cyclists have to wait behind a LMS Railway horse and dray returning to the Wicker Goods Yard. Tram 173 has just left the LNER Victoria Station shelter.

Looking towards Lady's Bridge on 14 January 1944 (opposite), with evidence of bombing in the area of the market and the site of the Brightside & Carbrook Co-op on the right. The still familiar landmark of the old Town Hall is seen on the left. The trams still look smart despite wartime austerity. Their white buffers were intended to make them more visible in the blackout.

Haymarket

A whole galaxy of trams, buses and cars, with hordes of pedestrians are crammed into Haymarket, looking towards the General Post Office in 1937. No less than fourteen trams can be seen — a sight to gladden any tramway enthusiast but perhaps not the traffic planners!

Trams ran on rails and were powered by electricity, for the electric motor was well-developed before petrol engines could be made sufficiently powerful for large vehicles. They drew their current from overhead wires, against which was sprung the grooved head fixed at the end of the trolley poles each tram carried on its roof. The electricity – at around 600 volts – then passed through cables to controllers (one at each end of the tram, but only one in use at one time) which regulated through resistances how much was passed on to the motors beneath the tram. All very simple, really, and efficient.

Fitzalan Square and Angel Street.

On 5 June 1937, the Sheffield City Engineer photographed Fitzalan Square (above), and captioned the photograph *'Confused traffic conditions aggravated by trams, horse-drawn vehicles and uncontrolled pedestrians crossing.'*

Looking at the scene today, one wonders whether the changes have improved this spot, trams apart. Was the demolition of Barclays Bank really worth it?

At the top of Angel Street (right), in 1930 can be seen contemporary fashions in dress and middle-of-the-road tram stops, with the soon-to-be-demolished Fitzalan Market behind.

City

In February 1954 (above) car 250 — bound for Firth Park via Upwell Street — waits in Exchange Street opposite the war-time shelter used by Rotherham-bound trams. On the left is Norfolk Market Hall — built in 1852 — with the original Town Hall of 1808 in the right background.

In the days of the trams it was they which dominated the centre of town; buses tended to be kept to Pond Street, Bridge Street and Leopold Street. Even today, most of the buses that run through High Street can trace their parentage to tram services. Car 197 reverses on Church Street to return to Crookes (left).

On Pinstone Street was a long, attractive wooden shelter and a special passing track for outwards cars to avoid hold-ups at this busy loading point, although neither of the trams (opposite) is using it.

Staniforth Road

Most of Sheffield's tram network was double track, but there were some sections of single track which allowed cars to travel in both directions along narrow roads. The unusual layout on the railway bridge on Staniforth Road (above) is of interlaced track with signal control, which saved putting in points. The bridge was widened in 1956, allowing just two years of normal tramway operation here.

Darnall and Handsworth

Darnall was a busy junction; this April 1957 scene, looking down Main road towards Sheffield (right), shows two cars passing Darnall Cinema, which is now a furniture shop. The tracks curving in from the left are from Prince of Wales Road and those to the right lead to Handsworth.

Main Road, Darnall (below), with car 119 climbing to Oliver's Mount. The houses are typical of late-Victorian Sheffield. In the background is one of the low-height AEC buses built in 1956 to negotiate low bridges in the Dinnington area. Darnall Congregational Church spire is also visible.

City Road to Intake

The domed-roofed cars were probably the most handsome trams produced at Queens Road Works. Car 300, built in 1939, leads a procession of vehicles up City Road past St. Aidan's Church in May 1952 (above). Note the impatient American car racing dangerously past in the wrong lane. This was a route for splendid views over the city to the western moorlands as the tram climbed the long length of Duke Street and City Road.

Manor Top (opposite) in 1954, with an interesting period meleé. A works service car is coming off Prince of Wales Road bound for Intake. AEC Regent bus no. 19 heads in from Eckington, with a SUT AEC Regal coach following. The Leyland PD2 bus (with *Trubrown* advert) is on the Outer Circle route.

The descent to Birley Vale (opposite) was a more rustic affair in January 1955, with many cottage rows, now mostly lost in over-zealous slum clearance. Tram 288 reminds us that trams were more reliable in snow than buses.

The unusual finger-post at Ridgeway was photographed in 1960 (opposite), four years after closure of the Intake tram route! It is now displayed at the Crich Tram Museum.

Heeley

At the start of the 1957 football season (left), a line of empty trams waits on Wolseley Road for the final whistle at Bramall Lane. There was no regular tram service on Wolseley Road, although the two loops of thick cable above the overhead wires show that current was fed into the overhead here (as it was at half-mile intervals throughout the system).

The imposing junction at Heeley Bottom (below) is crossed by car 256 on the last day trams ran between Meadowhead and Sheffield Lane Top via The Moor on 2 April 1960. In the foreground are the Wolseley Road tracks — not a proper intersection, for trams 'bumped' over the London Road main line. The view today, albeit without trams and with new obtrusive overhead equipment, remains much the same.

Chesterfield Road

Heeley Bridge (above), a scene familiar until recently. The *Palace* Cinema was demolished in 1982 whilst the station closed in 1968. Excursions to Scarborough and Skipton are offered. Another last day shot, with Roberts car 505 beginning the long climb to Woodseats. Under the bridge is an Atlantean bus of the type that had replaced the Woodseats via Queens Road tram route the previous year.

Tram 174 (right) reverses at Woodbank Crescent on the steep climb up Chesterfield Road to Woodseats on 2 April 1960.

STOP
HOME MADE
FAMILY BUTCHER
N. HUTCHINS

DOWN CARS
STOP
HERE

Woodseats, Meadowhead and Abbey Lane

Trams reached Woodseats via Abbey Lane or Chesterfield Road to either return to City, or continue up the hill to Meadowhead terminus. Car 72 is at the Woodseats end of Abbey Lane (left), bound for Sheffield Lane Top after completing its outward journey via Millhouses and Abbey Lane. Derbyshire Lane runs along the distant hill top. *National Benzole* petrol is on sale at the garage.

Pupils from Rowlinson Technical School make sure they catch car 21 at Meadowhead on 31 January 1956 (right). Would they run down the A61 today?

A rural view near Beauchief Abbey (lower left), with Sheffield's finest tramway reservation, built in 1927. The people living in the bungalows had only to step out of their front gardens to board the tram.

Both pictures opposite were taken by the City Engineer's Office on 24 February 1959, a few days before trams stopped running on Abbey Lane.

Millhouses and Beauchief

At Moorfoot in November 1958 (left), looking towards The Moor, where trams ran across the centre of a new roundabout. In the left foreground is a typical tram-stop and iron section-box, which supplied current every half-mile or so along the route.

The Millhouses and Meadowhead routes joined at Highfields Library (left). Car 201 is bound for Vulcan Road on 24 February 1959. Behind is new Roe-bodied Leyland PD2 bus 1160 in the Joint Omnibus Fleet, returning from its morning visit from Bakewell.

Millhouses terminus (right), with car 252 about to proceed along the its own reserved track beside Abbeydale Road South, whilst a similar car waits on the loop to return to City. A clock was once a familiar sight at all tram terminals. Tram 183 waits on the loop. Holiday traffic from the adjoining park was the reason for the elaborate arrangements here.

At Beauchief crossroads (right), car 89 is about to swing off the Abbeydale Road South reservation, over the railway bridge to join the Abbey Lane reserved track. On the left is one of the attractive 1930s neo-Georgian tram shelters designed by the City Architect's department.

These photographs were taken by the City Engineer's Department to assess the changes necessary when trams ceased running along Abbeydale Road.

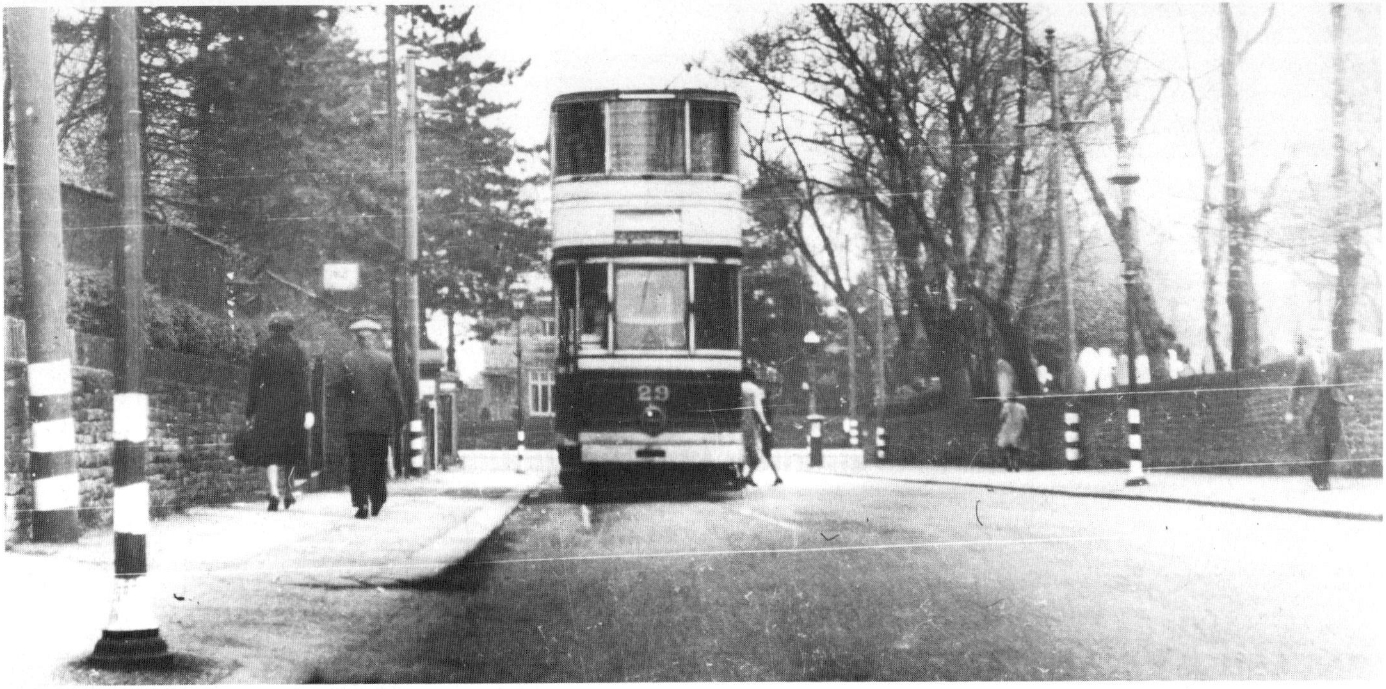
29

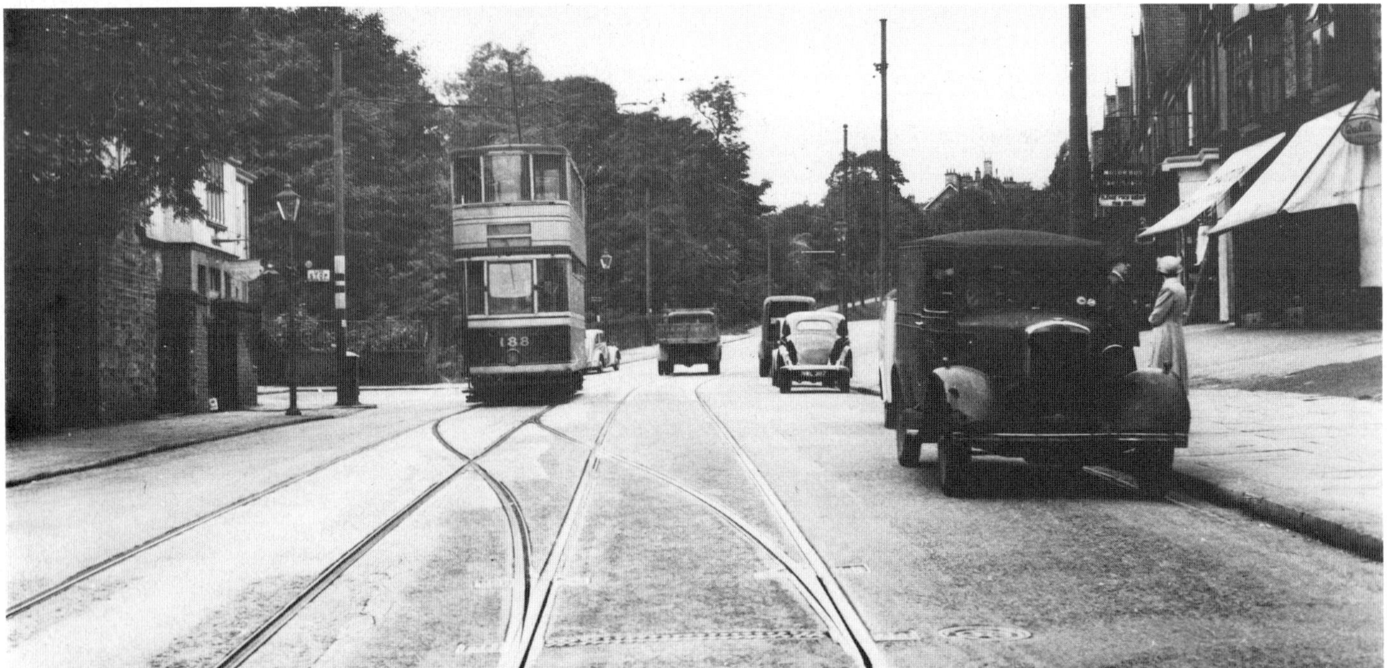
188

Fulwood and Ecclesall

Until 1936, trams ran to Fulwood via Hunter's Bar or Broomhill. By April 1940, only the Ecclesall Road/Rustlings Road route remained. Car 29 stands at the bottom of Canterbury Avenue at Fulwood terminus (left, top). The white bumper and masked headlamp and white bands painted on lamps and poles are all reminders of the effects of wartime blackout.

Car 188 passes the *Rising Sun* at Nether Green to proceed up the hill to Fulwood on 5 September 1951 (left, lower). Shaw's bakery van was a familiar sight in the district.

Standard cars 203 and 247 wait at Ecclesall terminus (above) at the top of Millhouses Lane in April 1940. The triangle of overhead wiring above the terminus automatically turned the tram's trolley pole. Cars would enter a terminus, pass under the triangle and then reverse out, pushing the pole sideways into the triangle beside the tram, then pulling it out afterwards behind them, ready for the next trip. In many towns the conductor had to 'walk' the pole round with a rope or bamboo pole.

Crookes

Crookes terminus (opposite) was on a bend, at the junction of Heavygate and Northfield Roads. Its location would today send a traffic engineer apoplectic, as would the elderly gentleman strolling nonchalantly along the carriageway towards car 245 in April 1957. A tasteful cast-iron traffic bollard marks the end of the line.

Tram 204 at the University stop on Western Bank in April 1957 (left), with the Children's Hospital in the background. In the foreground are the asphalted tracks of the Walkley route which had closed a year earlier, and which continued through what is now the Arts Tower car park.

Sheffield tram-drivers were able automatically to set track points as they approached them, by either drawing power from the overhead line as they passed beneath a contact, or by 'coasting'. At this junction, however, this useful practice was defeated by the rising gradient, so a pointsman was employed here to change the points until the route to Walkley closed.

Crookes Junction, Broomhill (left), with car 529 decending through the Victorian atmosphere this corner still somehow retains.

On the last night of the Intake-Walkley route in April 1956 at Manor Top (left), car 94 waited to descend Prince of Wales Road while car 505 worked inwards from Intake. Despite its destination – *INTAKE* – 505 is actually working the very last service from Intake to City.

During the 1950s some trams were experimentally painted green, but mercifully not for long. Car 216 stands in Weedon Street (above), near the end of a siding which allowed trams to wait off the main road – particularly useful at shift-changing times.

Every tram operator had works cars for those incidental jobs that would nowadays be done with a van or lorry. Generally they were economically converted from redundant passenger trams. In Tenter Street Depot stand three works cars (below). 330 began life as a Bradford double-decker and came to Sheffield in 1943 when the city was short of trams. In 1951 it was beheaded and fitted with an internal water tank. Car 354 was built in 1899 as single-decker 46, and in 1920 was turned into a snowplough — the blade can be seen beneath the platform. In 1960 it was restored to its original passenger-carrying condition and now lives with 330 at Crich Tram Museum. Car 352 was also a snowplough, but converted in 1927 from double-decker 172.

Walkley

War-time Walkley, (opposite). South Road at St. Mary's Church on 1 June 1940. Already, few people are carrying gas-masks, for this was the period of the 'phoney war'; six months later Sheffield was badly blitzed.

Car 217 surmounts the famous Barber Road 'hump' at Commonside on 28 March 1956 (above), bound for Midland Station, destination for about one in three cars from Walkley.

The *Harley Hotel* (left), at the end of Hounsfield Road took its name from the number of hospital surgeons who had consulting rooms in the adjoining terrace. Standard car 199 carries the older dark blue and gold livery, whilst 205 has the lighter cream and blue adopted after 1935. Once painted, cars were touched up and varnished, not re-painted, so the old livery survived to the late 1950s.

Hillsborough and Malin Bridge

Hillsborough Corner had one of the most frequent tram services in the City, for it was the junction of two routes, to Malin Bridge and Middlewood. All three trams at Malin Bridge terminus (left) in pre-war days were built between 1921 and 1937, when Sheffield was replacing its first generation of electric trams. Remarkably, the old forge on the left still stands, but the chimney departed in the 1950s. The Tinsley destination on tram 391 suggests a special works service.

On Holme Lane was a tram depot with a peculiar item of trackwork outside it. As trams could be driven from either end they simply reversed direction at terminals and used a crossover track to move back to the left side of the road. As crossovers 'trailed' beneath rather than 'faced' approaching cars, they only worked when needed. Outside Holme Lane Depot was a rare facing crossover to give access to the depot, which stood immediately to the right of the typical mid-nineteenth century three-storey tenements on the left side of the street. Hence the presence of a reversing triangle in the distance. Holme Lane Depot was also a regularly-used turning point for trams which did not need to go all the way to Malin Bridge or Middlewood.

Middlewood

Middlewood terminus at the end of hospital visiting time (right), with passengers queuing to board car 227. The shelter on the right still survives, but the replacement bus route was extended to serve the housing estate that now fills the fields beyond. The photograph was taken from the upper-deck of another tram.

Roberts car 536 was the last tram to be built for Sheffield. In March 1954 it was barely two years old as it turned left at Hillsborough Corner into Holme Lane.

Wadsley Bridge

The tram route to Wadsley Bridge followed the narrow byways of Neepsend, with glimpses of the River Don between ancient high-walled factories.

Deep inside one of Sheffield's industrial areas (left), car 272 negotiates the single-track section between the gabled factory walls and offices of the *Neepsend Steel & Tool Corporation* in September 1959. The line was protected by signal lights at each end; one can be seen on the pole at the left.

Not a great deal has changed at the junction of Nursery Street and The Wicker in the last twenty-five years, although Rip Van Winkle's excellent café has gone, a good vantage point to watch the passing trams. The food was excellent too!

Car 84 rolls down the hill from Wadsley Bridge in February 1954 (right), having just gone under the old Great Central Railway main line from Manchester to London Marylebone. The road here is now a dual carriageway, the stone bridge replaced by girders.

Hillfoot Bridge (left), built around 1885, makes a very attractive setting for Roberts car 536, which has just turned off Penistone Road in 1959. The cottages on the left have been demolished, but Jonas Woodhead's Clifton Works on the right still survives.

Football Specials reversing on Parkside Road (right) by Hillsborough Council School in March 1954. The trolley pole on car 376 is at the maximum extension as it turned on the special overhead reversing wiring.

Firth Park and Sheffield Lane Top

Trams reached Sheffield Lane Top via Barnsley Road or Attercliffe and Newhall Road, and the late war-time view, looking north from the terminus at Sheffield Lane Top (above), shows a selection of the 1930s corporation houses this route was built to serve. The central island and shelter are typical and date from the 1934 route extension from Bellhouse Road. Note the white-painted bumper and masked headlight on car 182, and the hood on the 'keep left' bollard, in case it was spotted by sharp-eyed nocturnal German aviators.

At Firth Park (right), car 102 takes the logical route through the roundabout on its way to City. The opening in the roundabout and the rails still survive, although trams ceased running in April 1960.

Car 75 (left) stands before Wicker Congregational Church on Burngreave Road. In the distance is the spire of All Saints, a landmark for many years. Like car 75, both churches have now gone.

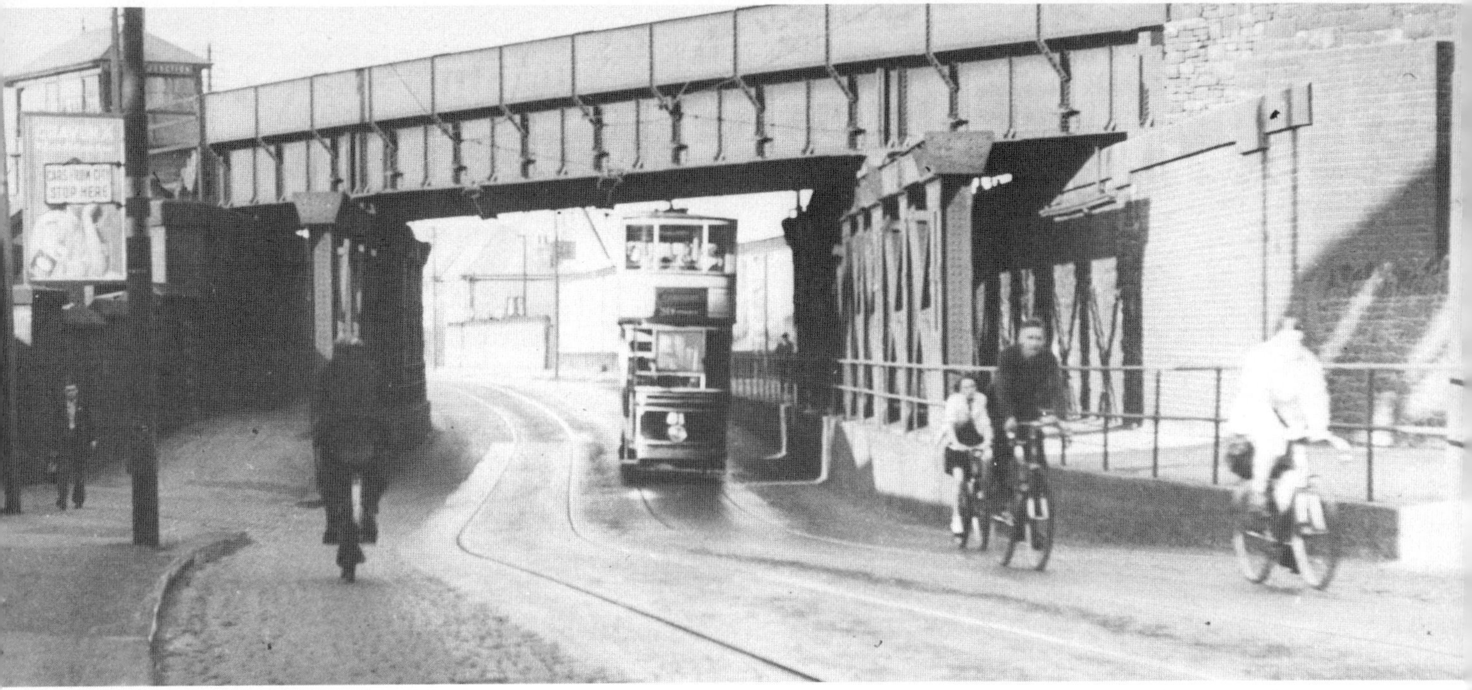
CARS FROM CITY
STOP HERE

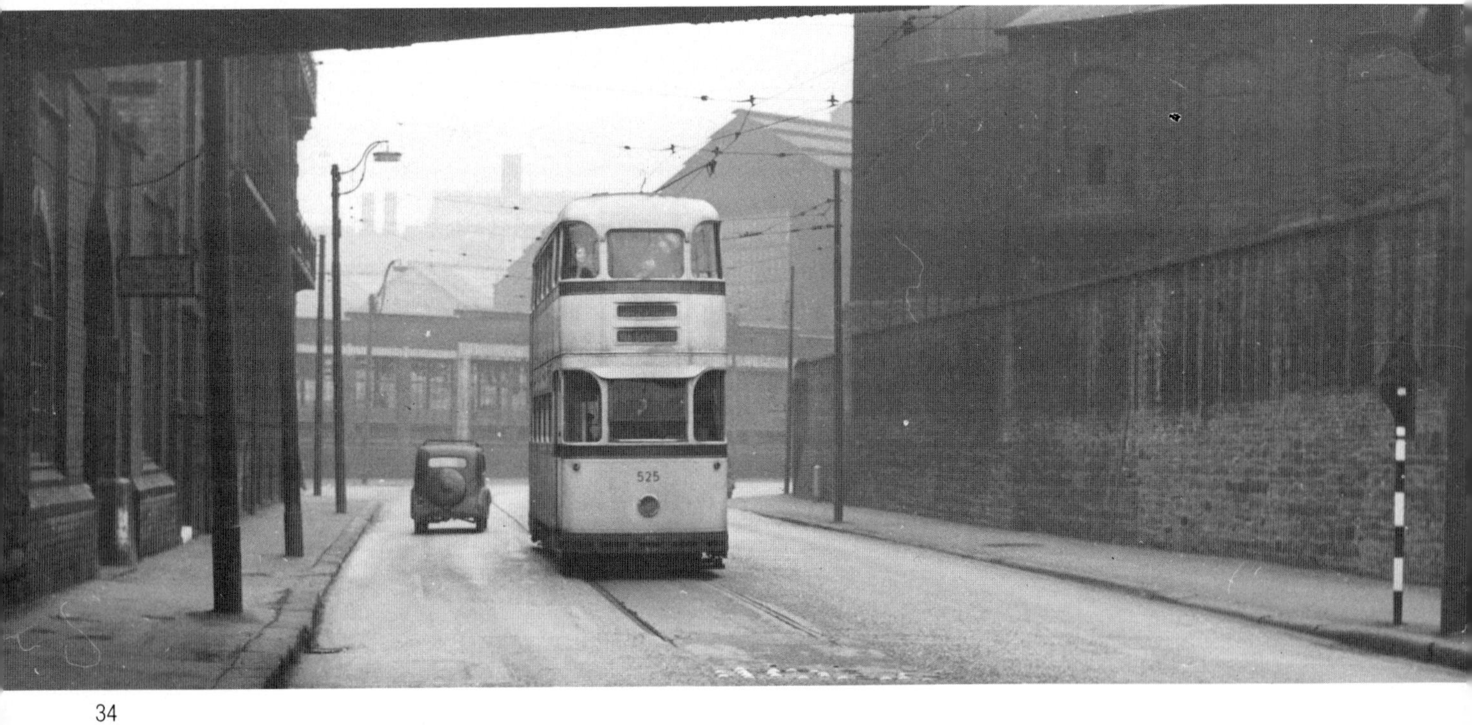
525

Brightside

There were two tram services to Brightside, apart from the works services which operated at shift-changing times, running to and from most suburban terminals. A direct service ran up Brightside Lane to the terminus at the end of Weedon Street, where it was always a welcome sight to see a car when returning from outside Sheffield – you felt you were home! A Roberts car stands at Brightside (left, below), over-shadowed by industry. The bridge was too low for electric cars to pass under, so the Brightside route was actually a few yards shorter than in horse-tram days.

'Out of the Cavern' (right). Looking from Upwell Street junction towards Brightside on a dull and cold last day of service in December 1958. A domed-roof car emerges from the gaunt brick walls of English Steel's *River Don Works*, having just crossed the railway linking the two works together. The triangular junction to the left leads along Upwell Street to Page Hall; the service along here lasted until the following February.

Brightside Lane in June 1939 (left, upper). Car 51 dips under the Midland Railway bridge, lowered to allow the passage of double-deckers.

The second service serving Brightside ran along Attercliffe Road, and across to Sheffield Lane Top via Newhall Road, Brightside Lane and Upwell Street. Car 233 coasts down Upwell Street in 1959 (right, above) towards the Midland Railway bridge carrying the line from Sheffield to Rotherham. In the early years of the route, only single deck-cars could be used because of the restricted height of the bridge, but the road was eventually lowered.

Attercliffe, Vulcan Road and Rotherham

From 1905 until 1948 there was a direct tram service from Sheffield along Attercliffe Common and through Templeborough to Rotherham. After Rotherham Corporation got rid of its last trams – some rare single-ended cars – in December 1948 the tracks went no further than Vulcan Road at Tinsley. On Frederick Street, Rotherham (opposite), car 165 is on the one-way track round the town centre. Above the tram is mixed tram and trolley-bus overhead wiring, with a single-deck Rotherham trolleybus ahead of the tram, beside where now stands Rotherham bus station. This was Sheffield's only 'joint' tram service and the only route extending beyond the city boundary.

A build-up of traffic at Staniforth Road Junction around 1957 (left). Once a busy and thriving area, this part of the city is a shadow of its former self. Happily, *Banners* soldiers on, albeit removed from its one-time eminence as one of the largest department stores outside the city centre. Car 159 stands next to a Duple-bodied Bedford coach.

The long double-track Vulcan Road siding at Tinsley was laid in 1927 and was officially termed 'works siding'. This allowed the works traffic cars from all over the city to load off the main route to Rotherham. Car 251 (left) carries tram enthusiasts to the gates of Hadfields *East Hecla Works*, where much of Sheffield's track and crossings were manufactured. The second track has already been dispensed with.

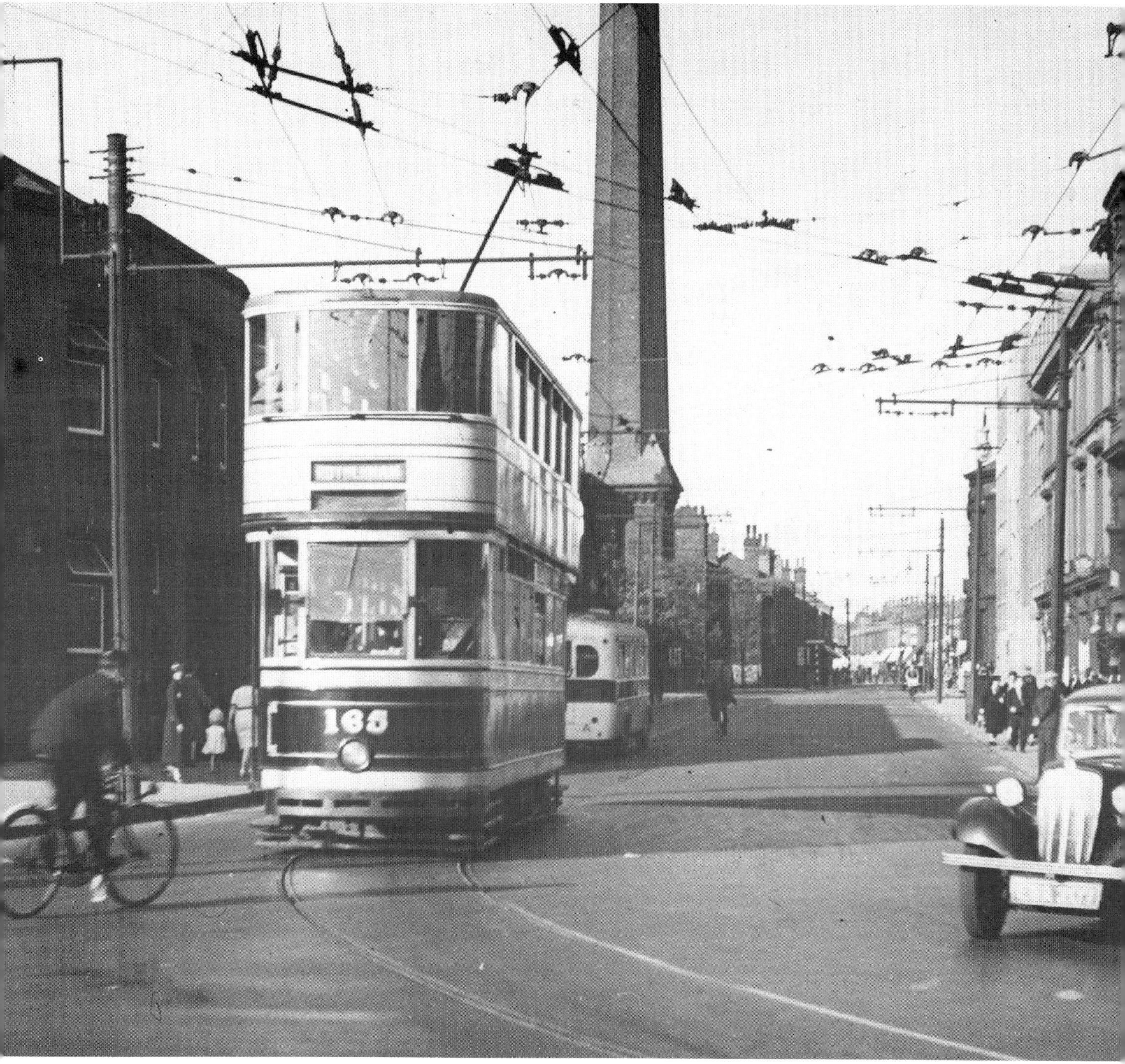
165

Moorhead and Fargate

Car 138 (opposite) about to run down Fargate and past the distinctive landmark of *Telegraph Buildings* to Marketside, the city terminus which was where C & A now stands. Although most tram services ran from one suburban terminus and through the city centre to another, it was generally necessary to buy two tickets, one for each section of the journey.

Jays furniture shop at Moorhead had what must have been the biggest fascia in Sheffield. This view (left) is looking across The Moor from Furnival Street (roughly where the dual carriageway Furnival Gate is now), showing the tram tracks that led off The Moor into Furnival Street at this point. Those from the right were not used, but those from the left saw trams occasionally.

There were a number of irregularly-used stretches of track in the centre of town which were sometimes useful, and the single-track line along Furnival Street, which car 278 is taking (left), was one such. On 17 May 1958, the Queen Mother visited Sheffield, resulting in cars normally travelling along Pinstone Street and Fargate being diverted away from the Town Hall into Furnival Street. Parked vehicles were a great problem here, but normally the owners had nothing to worry about – they probably had never seen a tram before on this little-used section of line. How very different is this part of Sheffield today!

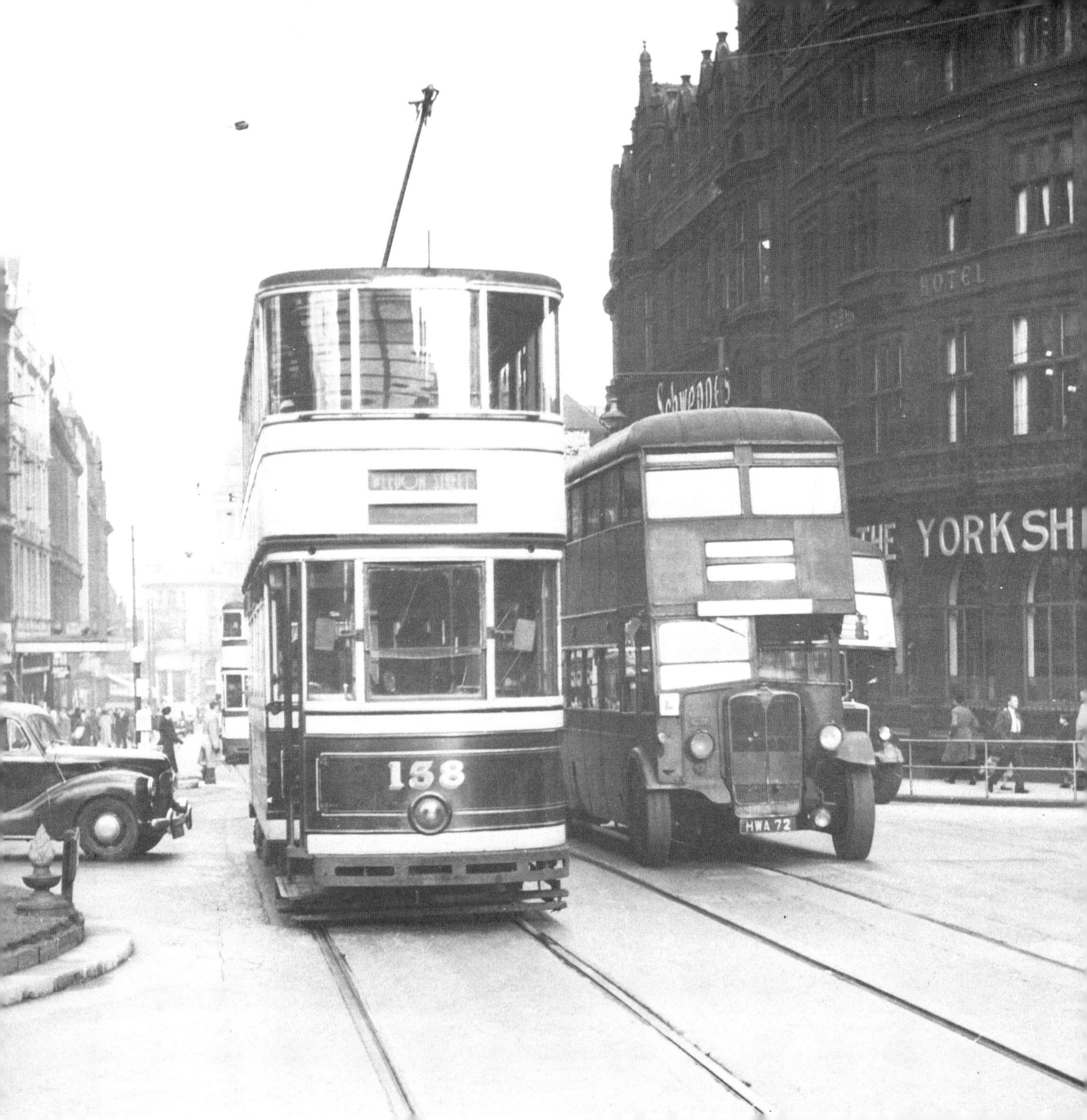
HOTEL
THE YORKSH
158
HWA 72

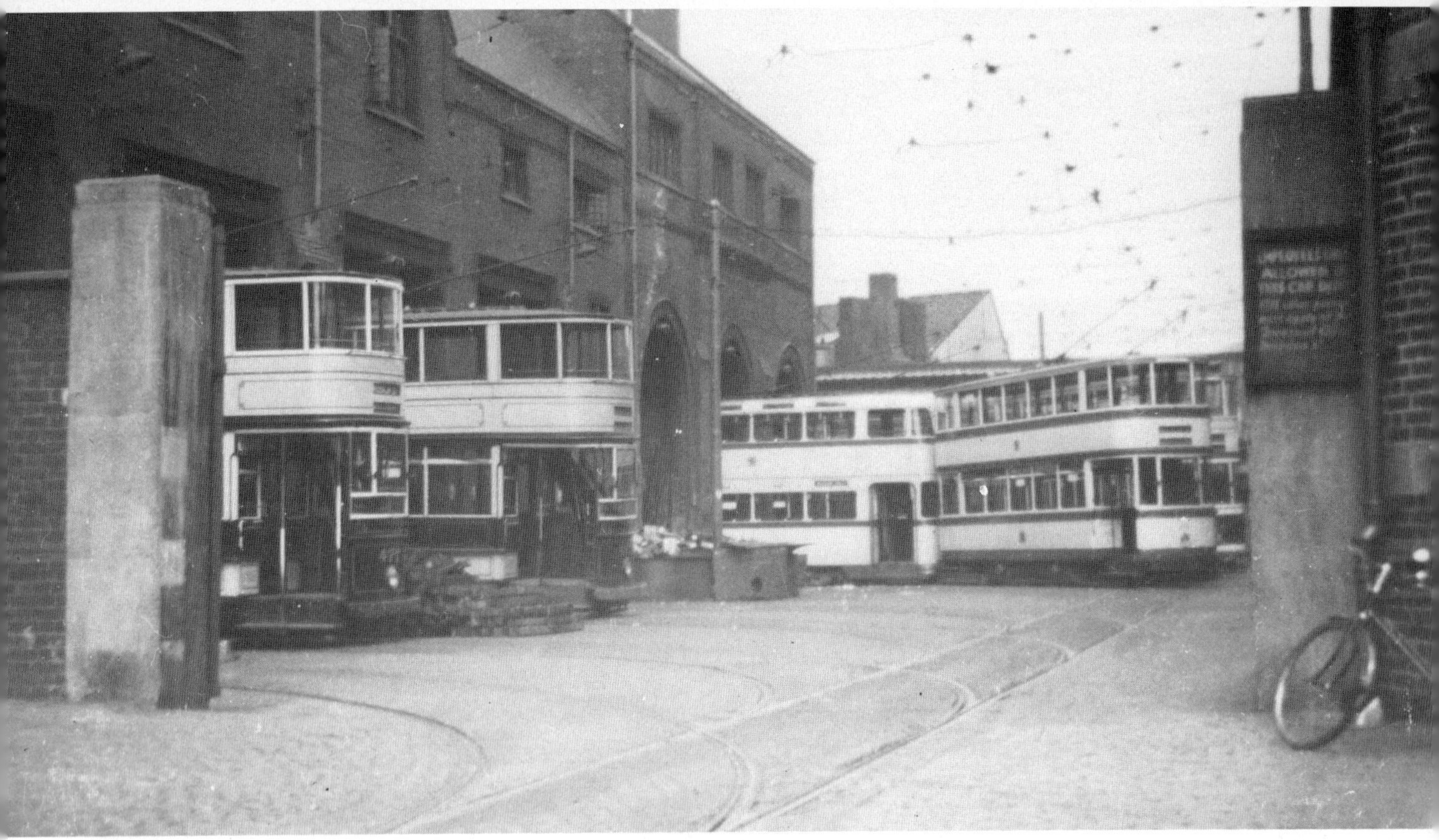

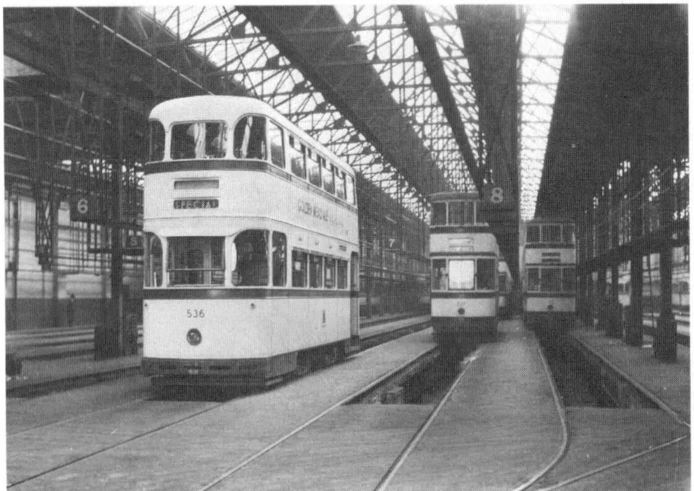
6
SPECIAL
536
8

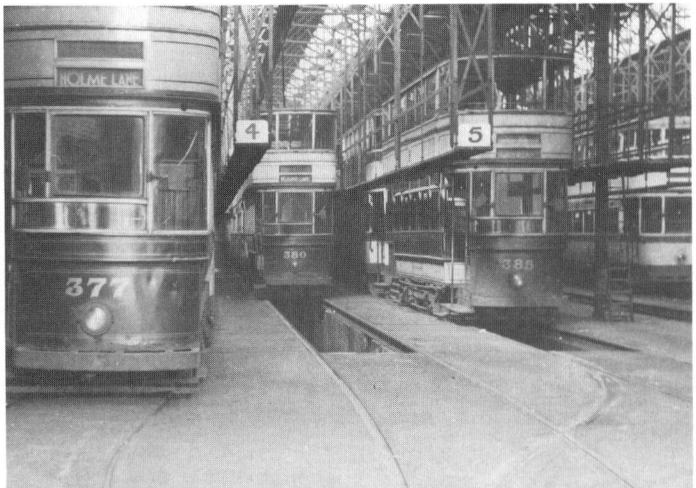
HOLME LANE
4
5
377
380
385

Depots

To house and maintain Sheffield's fleet of more than 400 trams, six depots were situated in various parts of the city.

Crookes Depot (above), was built to the designs of F.E.P Edwards, the City Architect, with *SCT 1919* inscribed in his typical Queen Anne gable. Car 200 is just entering in 1957. Behind the depot, on Fitzgerald Road, were built at the same time five corporation houses for depot staff. In 1938, Albert Howe, foreman lived at no. 10, whilst the others were occupied by tram conductors, a motorman and a storekeeper.

Over one hundred cars were kept at Tinsley Depot. On a Sunday in August 1952 (top, oppositet) the depot was full of cars not needed for service, with some outside in the yard for lack of covered space.

The very last tram built for Sheffield stands inside Shoreham Street Depot in February 1959 (lower left, opposite). A week later, the depot – Sheffield's largest – closed, absorbed by Leadmill Road bus garage.

Tenter Street Depot was the last to be opened, in 1928, and it was in use until October 1960. The Midland Bank block on West Bar Green was built on the site in the early 1970s.

Holme Lane Depot began life as a horse tram shed but was rebuilt for electric trams, continuing in use until March 1954. Tram 377 (lower right, opposite) stands beyond the fan of tracks that was required at depot entrances to take trams into the storage lines.

Queen's Road Works was the central overhaul depot for Sheffield trams.

Accidents

Trams had a deserved reputation for safety, for they were predictable and — as long as there were no leaves on the track — could brake very sharply. But they could not steer away from approaching trouble, and if the electricity supply was interrupted they were totally immobilised.

Car 217 has a spot of bother with a lorry at Ickles, Rotherham (left) in 1940. In attendance are the Sheffield AEC and Rotherham Bristol tower wagons. 217 was later repaired and ran until 1958, for it was wartime and Sheffield was short of trams to carry munitions workers.

Not so lucky 438 (below) was travelling down Chesterfield Road in 1950 when it suffered a broadside hit from a runaway van from which it did not recover, for brand-new trams were arriving in the city from Wakefield and there was no need to repair it.

Tracks and overhead

Although trams were vulnerable to wheels coming off rails and trolley-poles leaving overhead wiring, such incidents were rare in Sheffield, for maintenance standards were exceptionally high.

Wayward trolley-poles were normally replaced by the conductor, using a long bamboo pole carried beside the tram's wheels or found hanging from poles at junctions. Serious incidents required a tower wagon, and one such is seen at work on Suffolk Road (above).

Tracks required periodic maintenance and occasional renewal. A rail grinder smooths track on Abbey Lane in December 1958 (top right), powered by a cable hung over the overhead wire. Pneumatic drills reverberated along Ecclesall Road (right), near Ward's Brewery around 1920, when tracks were being renewed. The Tramways Department was responsible for the road surface between tracks and eighteen inches either side.

43

44

Replacement by buses

The City Council decided in 1951 to gently rid itself of its trams over fifteen years, but nine proved sufficient. Routes were closed and replaced by buses from 1952; by 1960 only four remained. But on the parts of the system that remained, life went on. A sign of the times was the rebuilding of Pond Street Bus Station in the mid-1950s, just after the photograph of the solitary tram (left) was taken in 1955.

In June 1956, forty-nine year old tram 342 (opposite) left Queen's Road Depot for preservation in London. It later moved to Beamish Open Air Museum, County Durham, where it was converted to an open-topper and disguised as a Gateshead tram. Happily, it is now being rebuilt as Sheffield 342.

Some tracks no longer required were removed, but most were just asphalted over. The scene on Duke Street (right) in 1956 shows why it was often easier to simply leave the track where it was.

As the trams' last days approached, several tours by enthusiasts took place, intent on covering as much as possible of the remaining tracks. One such tour visited Woodseats in March 1960 (below left). Various preparations were made to see off the trams; several were kept for preservation and stores car 349 (below right) was decorated as an open-topper.

8 October 1960

Sheffield's last tram service, from Tinsley to Beauchief, was run with cars from Tenter Street Depot. Tinsley Depot was simply a store for trams going for scrap, and Queen's Road Works was still in use. On Saturday 8 October trams ran out of Tenter Street just as they always had done, but from mid-afternoon, one by one, they disappeared into Tinsley Depot (left), where a small crowd of mourners was kept firmly out by closed depot gates.

Car 222 (below) was the very last service tram from Beauchief, but it left many disappointed passengers by the roadside, for it was full all the way to Weedon Street, Tinsley. Later that evening fifteen trams left Tenter Street and processed in pouring rain to Beauchief and back to the Town Hall (below), and then on to either Tinsley – for scrapping – or Queen's Road, for preservation. In that never-to-be-forgotten cavalcade were ordinary trams that had run in service the previous day, specially painted trams – including 510 with *SHEFFIELD'S LAST TRAM* marked upon it – and an illuminated tram and restored single-decker no. 46. Thousands of Sheffielders lined the streets that night, whilst those who were able rode out to Tinsley for the very last time.

Aftermath

Sheffield's trams were cut up and burned in Ward's scrapyard, just across the road from Tinsley Depot, where many cars were stored for their last weeks. The last tram entered Ward's on 21 December 1960, but the process had been going on since the Fulwood and Malin Bridge routes closed in 1952, the year that car 402 (above) was photographed.

Immediately after the last trams ran, work began on removing wiring and covering tracks (and the folk on Abbeydale Road South had parking places for their cars). In the Wicker (right) a new pedestrian refuge was put down on top of the rails. Wicker goods depot and Spital Hill are seen through the arch, along with one of those traffic jams which was supposed to have disappeared with the trams but rarely did!

Taking advantage of the tracks still being down, a special single-deck horse tram ran on The Moor for a short time in the run-up to Christmas 1961, but until Sheffield's new Supertrams appear in the 1990s, that was that.

What's left behind...

Although it's more than twenty-five years since trams left Sheffield's streets, they have left behind them a surprising collection of relics. As well as items that can be seen in Sheffield itself, several complete trams remain, operating in tram museums.

Sheffield closed its tram system at just the time that preserving trams was becoming a practical notion. A site for a working museum had recently been found at Crich, just south of Clay Cross, and in the weeks following closure it gave sanctuary to no fewer than seven Sheffield trams, including two works cars and a horse tram.

Double-deck cars 189, 264 and 510 can be seen at Crich, as well as single-deckers 15 (a horse tram) and 46 (electric). Works car 330 (which began life as a double-deck car in Bradford but came to Sheffield in 1943) is with them, but works car 349 was converted into a generator car soon after arrival and is now scrapped. Cars 510 and 330 operate at present, and 15 runs on special 'horse-car days'.

Roberts car 513 went into hiding for several years but ended up at the open-air museum at Beamish, County Durham, home also to Sheffield 342, which was first mutilated but is now being rebuilt to look as it should. 513 went on a working holiday to Blackpool recently.

At one time it was common for old tram bodies to be sold for use as hen-houses, games pavilions and summer-houses. Several old Sheffield tram bodies still exist in Lincolnshire, and part of one lingers still in Grimesthorpe. The body of 460 returned to Sheffield in 1987 after thirty-five years in the open air and is presently being painstakingly rebuilt in a corner of Tinsley Depot, with plans to one day run it on a length of track in Sheffield. In the meantime, however, Crich is the nearest place to experience the pleasures of riding on trams that once ran down Fargate and High Street.

But even if there's no chance to ride on trams in Sheffield, the City is littered with relics, some obvious, others less so. In Weston Park is an Edwardian band-stand bought out of the tramway profits, and on Upwell Street and Brightside Lane are railway bridges beneath which the road — but not the pavements — has been visibly lowered for double-deck trams.

At Firth Park, at the bottom of Bellhouse Road, there still lies a roundabout pierced by tram tracks, whilst on The Moor a short length of double line (and a section of pointwork) has been exposed to become the setting for two rather nice brick tram ends.

Much Sheffield tram track was left in place when no longer needed, and simply asphalted over. Periodically it re-appears as road surfaces wear or holes are dug. Odd lengths of track have been re-used for strange purposes, such as strengthening Corporation houses on Hands Road or edging beds in Whirlow Park. Some track (including a crossover from Beauchief) is still in use at Crich Tram Museum.

Heeley tram depot

Remarkably, all but one of Sheffield's electric tram depots still survive, along with most of one and part of a second horse-tram depot. On the right-hand side of Albert Road, Heeley, stands a brick-built horse-tram depot, with *1878* and *Sheffield Tramways Company* still carved over the entry arch. Although no tracks remain in the covered, cobbled yard, little imagination is needed to cast yourself back one hundred years. On Machon Bank Road, opposite Moncrief Road, a petrol station is built on the site of Nether Edge horse-tram depot (1877); part of the shed survives.

On Holme Lane and Pickmere Road, Crookes are recognisable electric tram sheds. Holme Lane, built in 1877 and rebuilt in the early 1900s, is undistinguished, but Crookes Depot is magnificent, with *S.C.T. 1920* inscribed above the main entrance, and tramworkers' cottages adjacent to it on Road. Perhaps the depot superintendent lived in one, rather as Station Masters once lived at their railway stations.

At the end of Weedon Street, built in 1874 and inscribed *Sheffield Tramways Company* is the brick-built Tinsley Depot, which originally housed horse-trams and went on to be an electric car depot and finally the last resting place of most Sheffield trams before they went over the road to die in Ward's scrapyard. Once again, beside it are three cottages.

Leadmill Road Bus Garage was once Shoreham Street tram depot; the buses joined later and over-ran the building in 1960. On the gable, above the rather clumsily filled-in entrance at the apex of the building through which trams once entered and left, is inscribed *built AD 1910*.

On Queens Road, with beautiful *art nouveau* lettering above the entrance proclaiming it as *City of Sheffield, Queens Road Tramway Depôt* is what was once a tram depot and finally the overhaul works for Sheffield's trams. Car bodies were being regularly built at Queen's Road Works until the early 1940s, and it was still working on trams in 1960, when it devoted itself wholly to bus repair and overhaul. It is now closed, but inside the building in 1987 were still lengths of track. A strange building, started in 1900 and subsequently extended, not always sympatheticallly, particularly as it aged. Cast-iron brackets with hooks are still fixed to the outside, where once they supported tram overhead wiring on Queens Road.

Easily overlooked is the solid brick-built Generating Station at Kelham Island, from which flowed electricity to power the first electric trams in 1899 and for many years thereafter. It is now home to the Industrial Museum.

Although the splendid tram shelter on Pinstone Street has recently gone, other more typical shelters remain, at Meadowhead, Nether Green and Middlewood. Modest timber erections, built around 1930, their Georgian window-panes have been boarded over and their bright blue and cream paint covered in a practical drab olive. 0pposite the Children's Hospital is a variation, timber on a stone base with fitted public lavatories.

At Millhouses terminus a large brick shelter with lavatories still stands at the end of the loop, and at Ecclesall terminus is a rustic timber shelter with lavatories, lay-by and shrubbery that was only justified by the fact that from 1921 until 1954 the Dore bus only ran from the end of the Ecclesall tram route. On the south side of Fitzalan Square is the base of what was once a long stone tram shelter.

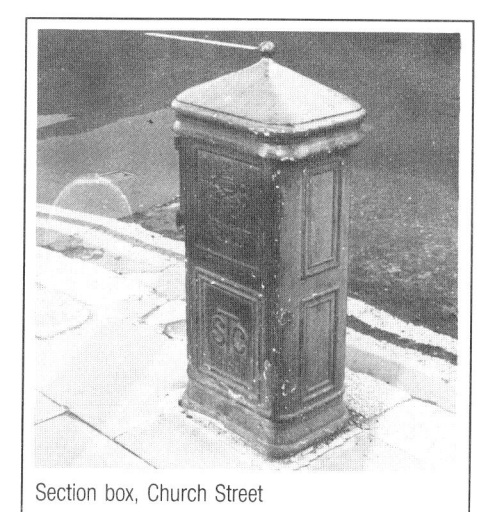

Section box, Church Street

Along tram routes cast-iron cupboards stood on the pavement, giving access to the electricity supply and a telephone, for power was fed into the overhead lines at half-mile intervals. At least two remain, one on Church Street, another on Prince of Wales Road, probably because leaving them is easier than removing them. They are embellished with an ornate *SCT* motif (for Sheffield Corporation Tramways).

Distinctive poles lined tram routes, to support the overhead wires, and in Sheffield they usually doubled-up as lamp standards, fitted with attractive iron brackets built around three circles of decreasing size. Few remain in 1987, but some still stand on Penistone Road (until the road widening is finished) and on Vulcan Road, where one has an interesting collar attachment that held a bamboo pole for turning trams' trolley arms.

By far the most common survivors are manhole covers, which lie quietly in pavements all

Manhole cover, Fulwood Road

over the City, thinking thoughts of long ago, when they gave access to the tram's electricity supply. A simple lid, with an iron frame surrounding concrete, four different types remain, two of which are marked with the maker's name: *Charles Ross of Heeley*. We have traced fifty-five examples. Their condition varies, for passing feet have worn them over the years

Two Sheffield pubs have signs that include trams, for no particular reason; the *West Street Hotel* and *The Tramway* on London Road. The pub that *should* have a tram on its sign but doesn't is *The Golden Ball* on Attercliffe Common — terminus of Sheffield's first tram route in 1873 — which has been recently renamed *The Turnpike* in that infuriating way pubs have of creating a new past for themselves whilst ignoring the history that really was.

A number of works buildings and sites in Sheffield associated with trams still defy Mrs Thatcher's economic wisdom and struggle on. Craven's on Staniforth Road once built tramcars. Samuel Osborne on Rutland Road produced *Titan* track, whilst Edgar Allen still successfully export special tram track-work, if not from their Imperial Steel Works on Vulcan Road, from Shepcote Lane. (In November 1987 *The Star* reported exports to Hong Kong and Canada.) Metropolitan Vickers made traction motors at their Attercliffe Common Works, built in 1916. In many parts of the world can still be seen tramway pointwork into which is cast the name *Hadfields*, and which was assembled at the recently-demolished East Hecla Works. Perhaps some of these manufactories will be able to supply parts for Sheffield's Supertramway when it opens in the 1990s.

On a lighter note, a glance in the window of Hibbert's Art Shop on Surrey Street will show how trams have affected at least one local artist. Many of George Cunningham's marvellous local paintings include trams quietly going about their business, often seen with a perception that isn't immediately obvious.

So, although Sheffield's trams have gone, they've left reminders of themselves. If any reader wants a complete list of the various sites the authors have located — or can point out anything they have missed — please write to them, care of the publisher.

Sheffield tram 189 is one of 210 standard cars built between 1928 and 1926; it is preserved with other local trams at the Crich tram museum. To its right on Penistone Road is a line of the poles with distinctive lighting brackets that supported tram overhead wiring all over the city; a few still remain.

It was in October 1960 that Sheffield said a reluctant good-bye to its blue and cream trams, after more than sixty years on the City's streets. This book takes you on a trip around the City in those far-off days of the 1930s, '40s and '50s, and tells you how Sheffield's tram system developed into one of the finest in the country.

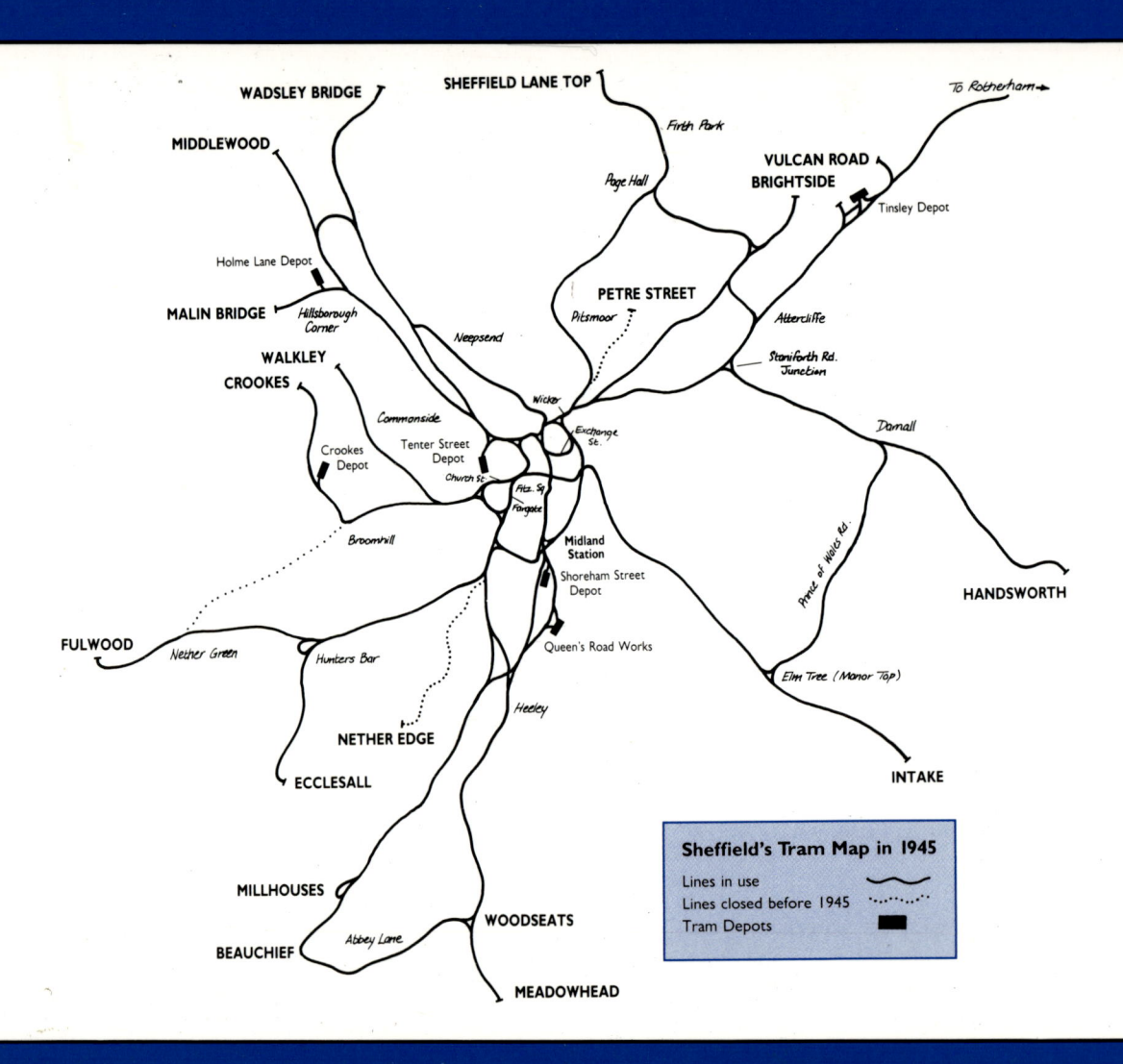

Sheffield's Tram Map in 1945
- Lines in use ———
- Lines closed before 1945 ·········
- Tram Depots ■

£3.25

ISBN 1 85048 006 0

SHEAF PUBLISHING